PIANO SOLOS

STRETCHING THE
STANDARDS

IMAGINATIVE ARRANGEMENTS FOR PIANO BY DICK HYMAN

ISBN-13: 978-1-4234-5504-2
ISBN-10: 1-4234-5504-5

HAL•LEONARD®
CORPORATION

7777 W. BLUEMOUND RD. P.O. BOX 13819 MILWAUKEE, WI 53213

Visit Hal Leonard Online at **www.halleonard.com**

PERFORMANCE NOTES
BY DICK HYMAN

These 12 arrangements are intended to depart a bit from the way that the songs were first set down by Irving Berlin, Jerome Kern, and Richard Rodgers. In terms of harmony, the use of modulations, and the recasting of melodies with unexpected accompaniment, I've tried, with all due respect, to move their classic songs into new territory. Sometimes I've embellished the melodies themselves in the way a jazz player might throw in variations, but these are not jazz variations. To the contrary, the settings are perhaps reminiscent in manner of some of the preludes of Chopin and Debussy, and of the shorter piano pieces of Ravel.

Many of the arrangements work best with a flowing, *legato* approach. On the other hand, "Hello, Young Lovers" has become a march for a phantom regiment, while "Lady of the Evening" dances the tango. Pedaling is occasionally specified but more often implied. In general, tempos are noted, but individual taste should determine the exact pulse.

ABOUT THE ARRANGER

Dick Hyman's multi-faceted career got underway in the early 1950s and has included piano-playing with Benny Goodman and Charlie Parker; arranging for Broadway, The Boston Pops, and numerous vocalists; artistic direction of many jazz festivals; film scores for Woody Allen and others; and over 100 recordings under his own name, including albums of the composers represented in *Stretching the Standards*. He continues to pursue an active schedule as a concert performer, often of his own chamber works.

PIANO STYLINGS OF DICK HYMAN

PIANO SOLOS

STRETCHING THE STANDARDS

IMAGINATIVE ARRANGEMENTS FOR PIANO BY DICK HYMAN

HELLO, YOUNG LOVERS

from THE KING AND I

Lyrics by OSCAR HAMMERSTEIN II
Music by RICHARD RODGERS

LADY OF THE EVENING
from the 1922 Stage Production MUSIC BOX REVUE

Words and Music by
IRVING BERLIN

middle pedal

sostenuto pedal

THE LAST TIME I SAW PARIS
from LADY, BE GOOD

Lyrics by OSCAR HAMMERSTEIN II
Music by JEROME KERN

LONG AGO
(AND FAR AWAY)
from COVER GIRL

Words by IRA GERSHWIN
Music by JEROME KERN

Moderato, freely (♩ = 92)

PEOPLE WILL SAY WE'RE IN LOVE
from OKLAHOMA!

Lyrics by OSCAR HAMMERSTEIN II
Music by RICHARD RODGERS

A little slower

Tempo I

THE NIGHT IS FILLED WITH MUSIC

Words and Music by
IRVING BERLIN

REMEMBER

Words and Music by
IRVING BERLIN

Andante, rubato and legato

THE SONG IS YOU
from MUSIC IN THE AIR

Lyrics by OSCAR HAMMERSTEIN II
Music by JEROME KERN

Andantino, rubato and legato (♩ = 80)

* *Bring out melody*

Bring out interior melody "A" and following.

*Bring out melody on F♯

* *Bring out melody in bass*

THE SWEETEST SOUNDS
from NO STRINGS

Lyrics and Music by
RICHARD RODGERS

middle pedal

THIS NEARLY WAS MINE

from SOUTH PACIFIC

Lyrics by OSCAR HAMMERSTEIN II
Music by RICHARD RODGERS

THE WAY YOU LOOK TONIGHT

from SWING TIME

Words by DOROTHY FIELDS
Music by JEROME KERN

WE KISS IN A SHADOW

from THE KING AND I

Lyrics by OSCAR HAMMERSTEIN II
Music by RICHARD RODGERS

46